# Missional Church

## What Does Good Look Like?



**Nigel Rooms**

Leader, Partnership for Missional Church UK,
Church Mission Society and Associate Priest,
St Peter's, Braunstone Park, Diocese of Leicester

**GROVE BOOKS LIMITED**
RIDLEY HALL RD CAMBRIDGE CB3 9HU

# Contents



**Church Mission Society supports the Grove Mission and Evangelism Series**
At Church Mission Society, we believe that every Christian is called to join in God's mission, whether that means crossing the street or crossing continents, and we want to set people free to put that call into action.




**First Impression** November 2019
**ISSN** 2399-6536
**ISBN** 978 1 78827 104 2

# Preface

This book completes a trilogy of Grove books on the subject of missional church. I began writing with Pat Keifert on *Forming the Missional Church*, a Grove booklet that described six corporate spiritual practices (or 'holy habits') that we designed to be faithful to the Christian tradition and disruptive of the prevailing culture in local churches.[1] We have also published on the subject of leadership: in *Spiritual Leadership in the Missional Church*, our main inspiration came from systems thinking.[2] This booklet looks towards the end of the process of becoming missional. When a local church sets out on a spiritual journey of discovery that aims at joining in with what God is up to (the *missio Dei*), the specific outcome cannot be defined. The journey is not a straight line from A to B. It is vitally important that churches who embark on this journey have some idea why they set out in the first place and bother to overcome the significant obstacles there will be on the path of change. This book will describe what 'good' looks like as churches begin to embody a missional vision, both for themselves and their communities.

**When a church sets out on a spiritual journey the outcome cannot be defined**

All the books in the trilogy have referred from time to time to a process of missional change called the Partnership for Missional Church (hereafter 'PMC'). What these books are definitively not, however, are some kind of promotional material for that specific way of becoming missional. It is simply that the authors' experience out of which they write is based in PMC. Though we hope these books will be very relevant for churches undergoing PMC, we have written them in such a way that any church could engage with the principles we outline. For that reason, I have included stories and voices from churches that have participated in PMC in each of the main chapters. I am truly grateful to each participant for their contribution. There is also a supplementary file of other testimonies available on the PMC section of the CMS website for readers who may be interested.[3]

In 2017–18, independent impact-evaluation research was carried out on over 80 churches across England who had participated in PMC since 2011. This included a survey sent to all these churches (whether they completed the process or not), which resulted in 109 individual responses from 53% of the churches. In addition, four case study churches were visited by the researchers. Since the people at Transformational Index who conducted that research were independent and have no vested interest in what they found, much of this book will draw on their findings through both the survey and the case-studies, which are publicly available in a 24-page report.[4]

# 1 Introduction: The Missional Church

What is missional church? This is a difficult question to answer, not least because it is mostly about the corporate *formation* of beliefs, attitudes, values, skills and habits arising out of and connected with knowing a few things well. We normally introduce the idea in the following way.

Being missional is more than just doing a few extra social-service or evangelistic activities or, indeed, increasing the membership of a church. Being missional affects everything that a church does and is. 'Missional' describes the character of the church. In a missional church, mission is not one among many activities. It is instead an intention that is demonstrated throughout the life of the church. A missional church looks for how *God* is in mission in the world today in light of how it knows God has worked in the past, especially through Jesus Christ. A missional church chooses to *join God in that mission in the world*, to let God call, gather, centre and send it in that mission. A missional church knows that a part of its calling is to catalyze in the world a glimpse of God's future, to be a sign of God's reign.

This places the journey to becoming missional firmly in the frame of the *missio Dei;* the theological assumption that before the church does anything God is already at work in the world in the overflow of God's love for that world (John 3.16).

This works out in practice in PMC in particular ways and perhaps it is best to let the Transformational Index (TI) report describe briefly what happens:

> PMC is a theological process designed to take churches on a spiritual journey in which they discover what God is doing in their context and what God's 'preferred and promised future' is for that church and community. PMC is not a 'programme' that a church can pick up for a quick-fix, it is a three-year process designed to help churches engage in new missional ways with their congregations and the communities they serve.
>
> At the centre of the process are six spiritual practices referred to as 'Holy Habits,' which churches are encouraged to engage with in order to discern what God is doing and allow space for God to speak and guide them; Dwelling in the Word, Dwelling in the World, Announcing

the Kingdom, Hospitality, Corporate Spiritual Discernment and Focus for Missional Action.[5]

The impact research presented in the TI report required a framework with which to evaluate PMC. TI worked on this with key stakeholders who came up with five indicators of transformation that define what good looks like in missional churches (hence the title also of this book). The five indicators, with my brief explanation, are as follows:

- *Inspiration*: Missional church is *first and foremost* about God and the movement and sending of God's Spirit. We expect to see God at work and join in—which is literally inspiring.
- *Engagement*: Missional churches proceed by forming relationships between actual human beings—those relationships begin with deep listening and therefore engage an other.
- *Empowerment*: If the Spirit is at work, we expect that people will have more agency to participate in God's mission and this will energize, release them and grow their faith in the God of mission.
- *Systemic change*: Missional churches do not change in straight lines, but, rather, through numbers of individuals becoming committed to a new way of being church. Over time we expect the whole system to change (including the wider church body that supports local churches).
- *Active learning*: We work with the action—reflection—further action cycle. Reflection and learning from lived experience (learning how to learn) is fundamental to missional transformation.

This book, therefore, fills out what good looks like under these headings in relation to actual churches with whom we have worked over the past several years. It includes voices and stories from these churches, both lay and ordained, which I hope will add colour and substance to the text. In the next chapter we will begin with God and inspiration. In chapter three we look at how engagement in God's mission leads to questions around witness and evangelism, and we suggest ways these issues can be helpfully treated in missional churches. Change and learning are always painful and that is the subject of the subsequent chapter as there is nothing programmatic or even magical about becoming missional—it is mostly hard work. Finally, we will look at missional churches' attempts to flip the clergy / lay relationship on its head, without underestimating the importance of clergy and leadership. All the main chapters end with a reflection question for you and your community to address.

# 2 God: Inspiring and Sending the Church

God who is three-in-one, community in God's-self, is our primary partner in mission. According to the theological idea of the *missio Dei,* God is up to something always and everywhere. This is not the place for a full-blooded defence of the understanding of how God is in God's very nature missionary, if by 'missionary' one means the eternal crossing of boundaries to the other in love.

It is worth dealing with one of the critiques of *missio Dei* here, though. Sometimes mission and the *missio Dei* can be used to justify any activity that looks vaguely positive in the wider community of a local church. This is not what we are talking about, since good missional being as church will always be *discerning.* Theologically God calls, gathers, centres and sends the local church into the world, not to get even busier but to discern where God is at work and become part of that. Discerning implies letting go of some activities and saying a definitive 'No' to other good things. We have spoken elsewhere of the importance of focus and not dissipating our energies into nothing, which according to St Augustine is sinful.[6]

Learning to discern as a church body (and not simply a bunch of individuals) is not easy though—it takes practice, and just like a toddler learning to walk there will be falling down and getting up again. The story of finding new partners from Nottingham at the end of this chapter is just one example of a church learning to discern.

So missional churches go looking for God at work in the world and this sets up a dynamic which was remarked on by the TI researchers in their report on the PMC journey:

> Our research has revealed that there is a three-stage cyclical process in the early stages of PMC. The first step is for churches to engage with their community, guided by the PMC process. This in turn leads members of the [church's engagement] team to be inspired when their efforts are seen to have impact. Inspiration again turns to engagement as others in the church and community can see the merits of the PMC process and the value of engaging with the wider community in new ways.[7]

We know from interview data we have gathered from churches joining at the start of the PMC process that, in general, their people display quite high levels of individual spirituality and even involvement in community outside church. What they hardly ever do is act corporately in public in the name of their church, authorized by the church council. The PMC process invites them to do this intentionally. Generally, such involvement creates fear and even a certain amount of terror in the teams set up to form relationships with 'people of peace' who have been identified in the community.[8] What is amazing is what happens when this fear is overcome and ordinary Christians realize there are people beyond their walls who, as neighbours, are waiting to work with them on initiatives they have discerned the Spirit is calling them to. The actualization of such discernment is inspirational for those involved and their new partners in the community. Such public action of the church thus makes a significant impact in the community for the good of everyone and becomes that sign of God's reign we referred to above.

When that inspiration happens, we encourage those involved to name the activity of God in public. We know from our research that the majority of Western Christians are practical atheists. This is not as shocking as it sounds. Ask most Christians the question, 'What is God up to?' and they will generally not start the answer with God as the subject of an active verb. That is, they will say what *they* have been doing or what the *church* has been involved in, but it seems we have trained ourselves out of the ability to name the activity of God when we meet together. However, when we start doing this, somehow the very life of God's Spirit is released in us (and thus we move to empowerment quite quickly). I have watched this happen many times—and it is often spine-tingling. Somehow it seems to me church and its activities crust over peoples' hearts as time goes by and they forget what it was that made their hearts burn to be Christian in the first instance. By allowing the naming of the activity of God it is as if that crust is taken away and their first love is rekindled. All mission begins and ends in the glory of God—good missional churches instinctively know this, can speak of it and act accordingly.

### 'How We Discerned What God is Up To'

St Barnabas Church, meeting in Thatcham Park School, had long aspired to have a community-to-community relationship with the school rather than simply through traditional activities. Our seven-year journey to learn how this happens has been enriched by PMC through partnership, community and hospitality. Two crises have helped us to see God at work and join in.

First a double booking for Messy Church and the school fete on the same Saturday became an opportunity when the church said to the PTA—'Why don't we do the food for you, and help with the stalls?' No longer a booking dispute, it became an opportunity to help the PTA, which was struggling a little at the time. We began to see how the PTA was touching the lives of our most needy families—and we saw God at work in that.

Then a mother was murdered one evening within sight of the school gates. Of course, everyone wanted to help and respond. We held meetings to pray and talk, there were conversations with staff, and lobbying—the immediate responses. The PTA arranged for Christmas presents for the children. The pastoral vocations of school, PTA and church became mutually visible, and there was a shared woundedness that deepened relationships. The need to grow support networks for adults in the community became obvious, and in the months following evolved into a PTA drop-in for parents, and ongoing support for pastoral staff. We are beginning to see more of God at work in the most vulnerable families in our community, who offer support as well as receiving it.

No-one would have planned either crisis. The three-way response to the murder was made possible by the trust and relationships that had grown from the response to the double booking—and it was certainly animated by noticing God at work in potential partners.

The Rev'd Mark Bennet, Team Rector, Thatcham, Diocese of Oxford

## 'How We Found New Partners in God's Mission'

In the early stages of PMC, we discovered that as a church, we needed to break down barriers inside and outside the church: barriers between old and young, rich and poor, well and sick, European and African, British and Asian, recent members and long-term members. PMC also showed us that we needed to be more outward looking and change our attitude towards the neighbourhood around us.

We thought that Slimming World, a group that used our church hall weekly, could be the partners that the Lord was directing us to, but they were not interested in partnership, so we moved on.

Next door to the church is Mellor's Lodge, a hostel for homeless families. Prior to PMC, this was just the building next door: we did not see the need to step out and develop relationships. The PMC practices encouraged us to develop a partnership with the management of Mellor's Lodge, allowing us to share the flow of God's love to a group of people who are experiencing temporary hardships.

Our changing attitude to the community outside the church enabled us to say yes when a wrestling club wanted to use our church hall for their shows. Over time, our relationship with them has grown, and we offer pastoral support in a prayer station and someone available to pray with wrestlers before matches or because of particular need.

The wrestlers have become our partners, and nationally the wrestling community refer to our church as 'the spiritual home of wrestling.' They even feel the place is blessed as they have never had a bad show here. They feel it is a nurturing place, so all new wrestlers perform their first matches here. Kevin, our community liaison, feels that Christian values have developed in the charity shows they perform to help others.[9]

Densel Davy, Reader, St Ann with Emmanuel Church, Diocese of Southwell and Nottingham

## Reflection Question

- How might your church answer the question—'What is God up to here?'

# 3 Missional Churches Create 'Public Christian Witness'

As part of the PMC process we ask churches to create a team of people who engage in ethnographic interviewing of a cross-section of their congregation at the start of the process (we referred briefly to this research in the last chapter). One of the optional eight questions that is asked is, 'Describe this congregation to someone new and tell how they would be nurtured here.' While writing this book I have been reading this data from these interviews. Despite differences of tradition and context, virtually to a church the responses to this question were much the same.

The churches overwhelmingly describe themselves through their interviewees as 'welcoming and friendly,' with one or two brave souls usually noting that after the initial welcome things get more difficult, especially if the newcomer does not quite fit the profile (age, social status, ethnicity) of the current congregation. This resonates with my experience that it is actually quite hard to join an average UK local church—despite the espoused welcome of virtually all of them. In addition, hardly anyone can speak of intentional nurturing practices for new members in the interviews. For the second part of the question the assumption hidden within the responses seems to be that nurture will be by osmosis—that is, as long as the new person is prepared to join in regular worship, social activities and perhaps small groups they will be able to be Christian and grow in their faith. Of course, sometimes the *Alpha* course gets a mention or even *Pilgrim* or *Start* courses, but it is clear that many, many church members have no sense of how to enable a curious stranger to find a Christian faith.

**Many church members have no sense of how to enable a curious stranger to find a Christian faith**

This fact is not really surprising when we think about it as many churches live within the assumptions of Christendom. Potential newcomers are in some way assumed to be already Christian or at least sympathetic and again just need to fit in with the way we do things. Over the past decades many initiatives have attempted to enable church members in what is sometimes called personal evangelism. I remember *Evangelism Explosion, Good News Down Your Street,* and creating your personal testimony to name but a few approaches. However, not much has changed. We have a hypothesis about why this might be related to the capturing of our churches in the Western world by the culture of modernity.

## Modernity and Faith

Such a culture, as well as muting us speaking about God, separates facts from values, the sacred from the secular and the private from the public. Religion in the Modern period (1650–1950 approximately) has become a value or an opinion which is relegated to the private sphere. Whether it is by having a personal faith in Jesus, with the intimacy that goes with that, or turning up at 8am every Sunday to 'make my communion' and leaving without speaking to anyone, the phenomenon is much the same: a privatized religion of the heart. There is nothing wrong with that, just that it is extremely limiting in that it remains largely in the private sphere. On the other side of the split is the public world which is the realm of hard facts and, since religion can never be scientifically proven, the public realm is mostly understood by Christians and non-Christians alike to be hostile to Christian faith. A gulf opens up between church and world and the church puts up its barriers to keep the world out (as in Densel's starting point in his story in the last chapter).

Evangelism is problematized, then, since there is little plausibility structure within which it can take place in public (the theologically necessary location for it). This became clear in one of the first evangelical churches to join the PMC process, which has been researched more deeply during their missional journey. Christians there were caught between the rock of knowing they ought to be doing more evangelism with a big 'E' and the hard place of fearing that it will just be a cheesy interaction about getting Jesus into a conversation—with no foundation in reality, plus all the guilt and embarrassment that goes along with either option.

None of this, however, stops God doing God's work in the world; it is just that it goes on unseen and unrecognized by many people within and without the church. The *missio Dei* is liberating for evangelism as it arises out of God's prior work (when reading Luke 10 people often take time to notice Jesus is the Lord of the harvest—Luke 10.2b—preferring to focus on the scarcity of the workers). Evangelism is, therefore, not about more and more busy activity in order to get people back into church. Neither does it seem to be having something material which we offer to others in the world, since we are sent out without 'purse or bag or sandals' (Luke 10.4).

The key move that missional churches make out of the *missio Dei* is to take the walls of the church down and begin to engage in their communities by discerning what God is already up to there and participating in that. This includes discerning 'people of peace' (Luke 10.6) and, having met them, we need to be much more guest rather than host, receiving their hospitality (Luke 10.7–8). And such community engagement is *public* engagement (Luke 10.9–11—the healing and announcing of the kingdom is in the town and its streets). As we said in the last chapter, missional churches act *corporately in public in the name of their church, authorized by the church council*. I have emphasized the end of that sentence as there are three key words in it: corporately, public and authorized.

Evangelism in missional churches takes its place within the formation of Christian *community*. The unique insight of Christianity is that God, while being one, is also a community of three into which we are drawn as both host and guest (*cf* Gen 18, the Rublev icon and the eucharist). The church, as the agent of the communitarian God, therefore acts through community and in community to form new community around God's activity in the world. Of course, individuals will need to make a public and personal profession of faith as they come, and should also desire to join in what God is up to, but this will never be separate from the whole community of God's people. We will return to questions around what this looks like later.

## Faith in Public

Christianity is a *public* religion and has been from the very beginning. Christ was crucified outside the city in a public place of execution and became Lord through being raised from the dead in direct opposition to the acclaimed public leader of the time—Caesar—who was supposed to be the only *kyrios* or lord in the empire. Luke's continued narrative in Acts shows how the apostles often come under pressure for their public witness. No wonder we find evangelism difficult when we stop acting in public in the name of the church.

Thus, *authorization* is key—the leadership of local churches is expressed through the church council. The governing body of the local church is just that—a body made up of actual bodies. Those bodies authorize other bodies who are members of the church to go in apostolic faith to meet God in the world, in the strangers they will find.

The combination of these three things creates, I believe, the conditions for authentic (and what we might call post-colonial) evangelism in our contemporary world. How this works out is demonstrated by the TI research on PMC:

> We can therefore say that PMC has helped participating churches to explicitly name God in the local community—faith has made its way outside the church and, in some cases, this has resulted in people responding to it. This complements the evidence of people reporting strengthened discipleship, as it is reflected in collective and individual behaviour. Given that this report has already identified increased levels

> of engagement and partnership, it follows that PMC has, in the majority of cases, led to a more *public Christian witness* and therefore evangelism. Significantly, there are signs that communities are positive about these interactions.[10]

Good missional churches take public action in the name of the church, creating a credible and plausible space within the community for conversations about faith that cut through the rock-and-hard-place dilemma of many Christians. Listen to this anonymous respondent also quoted in the TI report on the same page:

> I now feel far more confident when sharing my faith within the mums and babies group I have helped to set up and to run. I feel that this group is, for many mums, their church experience.

See how the speaker seems to realize that her church now has her back when acting on their behalf in public, such that there is a renewed confidence to speak of her faith. She is not alone, but rather as part of a community can speak out of the strength of that community.

Two caveats remain about how evangelism in missional churches works out. First, I believe we are consciously incompetent on how to walk with adults to a public identity in Christ, as we sometimes put it. Our world has changed beyond all recognition and our public identity now, as marginalized Christian communities in a largely secular culture, means the nature of catechesis and initiation needs to be reimagined. Some people are working on this and of course intentional nurture and discipleship courses like *Alpha, Pilgrim* and *Start* will be part of that. And there is much more to be done.

Finally, there is good evidence that in the Western world it takes on average four years for someone without a Christian faith to find one.[11] The research also shows that conversion, as we have affirmed here, most often happens in community through family members or close friends. This implies staying in relationships with a large number of people on a journey that for many may never result in a faith commitment. It thus stands against any attempt to grow disciples quickly. If, as in the PMC process, it takes 3–5 years for the walls of a church to come down and for meaningful relationships to be made in public then it is going to be 6–10 years before any of those may turn into significant numbers of new Christians.

### 'How I Shared My Faith as a Result of PMC'

I have always struggled to share my faith, trying to judge those supposedly right moments where your faith can be shared, and conversion happens! It has not felt right for me, and I guess deep down I have always felt a failure!

PMC turned my ideology of evangelism on its head. I didn't need to try and run around converting every conversation I had into a 'God' conversation! PMC made me stop, reflect and realize that God had gone before me. Instead I looked for those places to which God was calling me and ultimately the people God was calling me to, my persons of peace as we see in the Luke 10 passage. My weeks became an adventure! I was free from the burden of feeling like a missionary in the Victorian era, inflicting my faith on the heathen!

Just over a year ago, my husband and I went to a street party, a bit apprehensive, but feeling it was right to connect with the community we live in, to look for persons of peace. We met a group of people from five houses in all, who were isolated from the community. We were all of one mind that we wanted to connect, and so a group was easily formed. We decided to take it in turn to meet together regularly for food and hospitality. And the journey continues, sharing lives together, through redundancy, through illness, through death and new life.

This encounter has changed me and my family. I offered food for a neighbour as his father lay dying, something I more easily did for people at church. People have shared their stories, and together we have all found help and support. One of the group suggested we all went together to a carol service, and we did. The emphasis is not on me, God has gone before!

I see our group of dear friends being all of one mind, and my hope is that together we find faith in Jesus, in God's time, not mine. They are the people that God has called me to and tasked me to pray daily for.

Wendy Cranefield, Churchwarden, St Wilfrid's, Wilford, Diocese of Southwell and Nottingham

## Reflection Question

- What public action might be authorized by your church council and who would you authorize?

# 4 Change: Unlearning, Experimenting and Learning

All change is painful, slow and difficult; just think back to the experience of being a teenager. The process of becoming missional as a church requires letting go of one kind of identity with the long-held beliefs, behaviours and sometimes precious projects that go with that identity—unlearning. We explained in an earlier Grove booklet, *Forming the Missional Church,* that we are addressing deep cultural change and attempting to overturn centuries of ingrained habits that used to work well for us and now do not. As part of the PMC journey we therefore introduce the six faithful and disruptive spiritual and missional habits mentioned in our earlier booklet, and we watch how they slowly diffuse through the membership.[12] In our theory of how change happens following Everett Rogers, we expect resistance and even opposition, and that is almost as good as the adoption of the practices as it means they are being carefully evaluated.

If that was not enough, waiting for a new identity to emerge takes time and cannot be rushed; it requires experimenting and trying out new ways of being with God and the world (see the story from Charlotte Bolton below). As we remarked at the end of the last chapter, we believe authentic, sustainable church growth is both possible *and* slow in the world we now live in. In all this time of waiting the deep cultural drag or current to return to the old ways and habits is very strong, especially in crisis (*eg* a change of clergy leadership).

**Authentic, sustainable church growth is both possible and slow in the world we now live in**

In the second year of the PMC process we ask churches to experiment and create new missional partnerships in the name of their Christian community with people who are not part of the local church. This requires the team undertaking this task to go to places they have not been before and meet those they do not know without a sense of what will emerge—other than that God is at work in the area of engagement that has been discerned for the experimenting. We know now that this task of acting in public in the name of the church is pretty terrifying. Some churches will find any kind of displacement activity to avoid the task in hand—not unlike teenagers getting down to revision for exams! We think Charles Taylor's theory of the 'buffered self' in late modernity helps us to understand what is going on here.[13] Western people, again because of the effect of modernity, have buffered themselves not only against the world of the spirits, of heaven and hell, but against each other as well. Add in the belief that the secular world is somehow against the church, and that people outside the church naturally suspect Christians of only wanting them as pew-fodder, and we have a toxic mix that militates against the two-way 'prophetic dialogue' required in authentic mission and evangelism.[14] Most of the practices in PMC are designed to help Christian people engage and therefore make tiny relational steps towards the other. Such steps, like stepping stones in a river, need to be just far enough apart to feel safe each time—for both sides.

Overall, then, becoming missional as a church is a liminal movement from one state of being (or formation, to use theological language) to another. One of the best ways to describe such a movement is with Theory 'U' popularized by Otto Scharmer and others.[15] There is a movement down the left leg of the U (which in PMC is years 1 and 2) as churches arrive where they are in their stark reality and begin to realize the difficulty of experimenting to discern their future with God. There really is not a short cut across the top of the U—just as it is not good to go straight from the hosannas of Palm Sunday to the joy of Easter Sunday without experiencing the depth of Jesus' passion in Holy Week. In fact, somewhere towards the bottom of the U there is a moment of desolation (equivalent to, of course, 'My God, My God, why have you forsaken me?'—see also Phil 2.5–11) which we have to go through if the new is to come. And in reality, there may be multiple such moments through which we keep having to be held on the journey. We connect here very closely with the methods of pioneer ministry and fresh expressions of church. I know a pioneer leader who said he conducted between eight and twelve failed experiments over five years in the community he was sent to start something new in. He almost gave up but then the new thing finally emerged from the tatters of what had not worked.

Some churches, therefore, for a variety of reasons, do not make it to the end of the PMC journey,[16] since there is nothing magic or programmatic about a change process like PMC.[17] When churches wish to leave the process the leadership task is to share openly and non-defensively the reasons churches give for not wanting to continue. Often many of the other churches agree with the reasons given, but the very act of the discussion about leaving strengthens their resolve to stay with the process. They become more committed, not less, when they see others leaving.

Good missional churches that do emerge from the process have learnt how to learn, *ie* they can try something and even if it fails, perhaps especially if it fails, learn from it and try again. Such missional learning involves new language (since language and culture are very close), risk-taking and making swift, responsive changes of direction where necessary—certainly not in the imagined straight lines of programmatic approaches.[18] One of the five key elements of the impact evaluation framework that we created with TI is *active learning*. We state the following axiom over and over again in one form or another in the cluster events: 'No-one learns from experience. We only learn from experience what we reflect upon and articulate to another' [in writing, drawing or speech]. The movement between action and reflection, encapsulated in the term *praxis,* coined by Paulo Freire and others, is deeply embedded in all we do in creating missional churches.

Becoming a missional church is not easy. Many of the participants will testify to that, but when we are caught up in discovering and discerning the activity of the living God and joining in with that work the difficulties and obstacles find their proper perspective. We are able to see them for what they are and go through, above, under or around them with joy and courage derived from faith.

## 'How We Failed Excellently and Learned'

We had originally thought our missional experimenting would be focusing on children and families, but some way into the process we realized that this was actually a technical and not an adaptive challenge; it would not change us. I really felt God was leading us somewhere else—I have never felt such a clear direction. We had failed to see how God was calling us. So we made the painful decision to change our focus and listen to the community feedback which said the church needed to come out from behind our churchyard walls and to take into account the evidence which told us that the ethnic make-up of our community had changed significantly; more than 65% of the people around us adhered to faiths other than Christian; the parish has a majority of Hindus, Muslims and Sikhs. We came to believe that God was and is calling us to build local community by developing graceful relationships with our neighbours of different cultures. So here comes the trust—we had to trust that we had heard God speaking to us as we went through the next year of preparation—asking people to speak to their neighbours about their faiths. We trusted in God and decided to put on our 'Festival of Season's Greetings'—the members of the PMC steering team led by example and made personal contact with their own neighbours of other faiths, talked to them about their festivals and asked them to come along with a display. I believe that the festival was a small but powerful step forward on our journey to finding God's preferred future for this church in this community. I'm proud to have been part of the festival. I'm proud that people were stopping us in the street and saying good things about our church. I thank God for all that.

Viv Froggatt, Reader and Community Development Officer,
St Mary's, Humberstone, Diocese of Leicester

## 'Why It's Worth Persevering with PMC When it Gets Tough'

In the second year of our PMC journey the MIT (Mission Innovation Team) was introduced as a kind of research and development team and it seemed a straightforward exercise, or so I thought when I began to convene it! Develop objectives, design protocol, experiment, get results, interpret and disseminate. My day-to-day job includes research and I frequently speak to people at times of their vulnerability through a healthcare role.

MIT experimenting puts the whole team into what felt like a washing machine and the specific wash programme has to be gone right through. You also need wisdom, particularly to translate the jargon in the instruction manual. If only it was as simple as pushing a button! At times, you wish you could open the door and climb out to get on with it, but in order to achieve the result, the wash cycle needs to be completed. The MIT process can be a turbulent ride, exposing vulnerabilities through challenging conversations and ways of thinking. There are essential ingredients including people of peace, clergy, PMC steering team and leaders; human interaction is key.

On completion, you come out spiritually refreshed; far more willing to stand up in the name of Jesus with conviction to share your story and to integrate your Christian faith fully into other aspects of life. I was never embarrassed by my faith but recognize now it was like a handkerchief (often tucked away but essential and close at hand) rather than a newly laundered shirt: clearly on show and defining who I am.

The MIT work allowed us to experiment *on projects* we discerned, but we worked hard to ensure we did not experiment *on people*. Yes, we had the occasional excellent failure and at times came out bruised. But bruises soon heal, and we have learnt and shared the journey. As a result, we, and many in the church community, have a clearer perspective and deeper understanding and motivation for our mission. Are we committed to working in partnership and '*Living for Jesus*'? —you bet![19]

Prof Charlotte Bolton, St Leonard's, Wollaton, Diocese of Southwell and Nottingham

## Reflection Question

- How might your church habitually learn from experience—especially your failures?

# The Future of Missional Church is in the Laity

5

A caricature of the life cycle of local churches goes something like this. A new minister arrives and everyone is full of hope for the new ministry. The clergyperson, after a brief period of listening, goes up the mountain to receive the vision of God for their congregation(s) and shares it as widely as possible. This plants some kind of flag in the future to which everyone is encouraged to move towards over the next three/five or even seven years. The leader's task is understood as bringing the people along to align with the new vision. The years pass and somehow the future that was presented is never quite realized by enough people, the leader moves on and the whole cycle repeats itself. The deep culture of the church stays much the same.

While this is a caricature or cartoon picture of what happens, there is much truth in it. Missional churches change the usual relationship of clergy and people. We have written elsewhere about how to understand the leadership task and will not repeat here the ideas presented there.[20] Suffice to say I absolutely believe in the importance of leadership but not in what Keith Lamdin has termed the 'monarch' (a single person rules) or 'heroic warrior' ('Follow me over the top everyone!') styles.[21] What I have come to believe from both research and experience is that it is God's people who hold the future of their local church in their hands.[22] Research shows that a small number of people (around 5–15 at the most) are at the core (or inside family) of all local churches and it is these people who hold the very long-term interests and vision of the congregation in their hearts, minds, souls and bodies. Sometimes that which they hold is explicit, energizing, life-giving and infectious and sometimes it is mostly the opposite of those things. When we think about it we know instinctively this is true since clergy come and go and some try to make their congregation in their own image, only to find a reversion to type after they leave.

**It is God's people who hold the future of their local church in their hands**

Good missional churches therefore discern, hold to and live out a vision for embodiment that becomes embedded in the key laity of the congregation so that it can endure beyond temporal changes in clergy. Many churches have a mission statement, but it is not much more than a statement. It does not inform the day-to-day missional living of the congregation; it is not able to be embodied as they go about their daily lives as detectives of divinity, looking for what God is up to. This is not the place to work out the detail of discerning such a vision, but notice one thing. In the PMC process the visioning comes *at the end* of the three years and not at the start. The vision arises out of the stark reality of where the congregation is at and its experiments with its community. Only out of this difficult and tough journey, as we have seen, can a new vision emerge—up the right leg of the 'U' movement. And sometimes movement out of the liminal 'U' can be very fast. We saw one benefice create their vocation statement in about five minutes and everyone in the team knew it was exactly the right one for them and it fitted what God was up to amongst them perfectly.

The TI impact evaluation report underlines the importance of the emerging vision at the end of the process:

> Participating churches have a clearer sense of their vision and purpose for their neighbourhood…Survey responses also confirmed this: when asked if they were more aware of their church's vision and purpose for their neighbourhood, 36% said that their awareness had grown to the extent that they can share it with others and a further 41% reported that it had grown significantly. Interestingly, churches valued vision being left until the third year of the process. It seems that vision has tended to emerge from experimentation and engagement, and perhaps is more deeply held as a result.[23]

## Empowering lay people

How, then, does laity empowerment come about in good missional churches? It starts by inviting them into public roles and teams within and outside the church, always supported, held and encouraged by the clergy, but not led by them. We saw in chapter two how inspiration and engagement were tied up together in a virtuous circle which also led to empowerment. In relation specifically to PMC, the six spiritual practices are designed for empowerment of God's people in the congregation. A good example is the core practice of Dwelling in the Word.

Dwelling in the Word is a group spiritual practice that can stand alone or begin a meeting, for example the church council. A Bible text (the same one is used for this practice for a full year across the congregation) is read out and each person notices where their attention is drawn in the style of *lectio Divina*. The twist is that each person finds a reasonably friendly-looking stranger and listens to what they noticed in the passage. This is shared in a larger group of four or six or even with the whole group. A *discernment* conversation ensues about what God is saying through the text to those gathered. It is clear to me that this practice is a fractal or microcosm of the whole move to become missional because, for instance, a private 1:1 conversation is then made public—the key move churches in modernity have to make. Therefore, there is resistance to this practice and here is a story from my own experience of leading a church through missional change (and which harks back to the bottom of the 'U' we described in the last chapter):

> After a couple of years of using the Dwelling in the Word practice at the start of church council meetings we had a mini-rebellion. A member of the council said, 'It's too hard. It's too hard to listen to someone else and it's too hard to get something from the passage each time we read it; me and my friends we want to stop.' Having tried very unsuccessfully pushing back to the person and having an ineffective first discussion about the practice we did that classic move and put it off until the next meeting, at which I knew this was make or break—the liminal moment! I asked everyone their experience of Dwelling in the Word. The person who had come to me repeated the objection with, it turned out, her friend in the singular. Another member said that for various personal reasons the dwelling practice had completely transformed her relationship with the Bible; she thought it was the best thing we had ever done. Other people were somewhere in between these two views, but were mostly positive. Eventually Christine, who gave me permission to use her name when telling this story, said, 'Well, it was hard for Jesus; he died on the cross why wouldn't it be hard for us?' That night some kind of dam broke in the council meeting and within a year or two we had a multicultural council which reflected the changing nature of the congregation. And we had fun at meetings because somehow God, and what God was up to, seemed more available to us than before.

Dwelling in the Word is a shared, liberative and ultimately egalitarian practice in which everyone's voice is heard, there is no expert who can give the definitive answer (though expert voices are not excluded), and corporate *discernment* wisdom is required to make sense of the room (or indeed the Holy Spirit's action on the room—*cf* Acts 15.28). Such liberation is echoed by the TI research:

> Our research has highlighted that empowerment of the laity is a significant outcome of PMC in the UK. For example, amongst our survey respondents, 76% had taken on new roles or responsibilities to those that had not (83:26 respondents). When asked about the type of role taken on, survey feedback showed that these included:
>
> - 37 directly linked to PMC, *eg* steering group, MIT, etc.

- 40 directly linked to the church—office holders, supporting administration, new groups, etc.
- 17 in the community—school governor, homeless initiative, etc.[24]

Such liberation as we have posited occurs through the six spiritual practices or holy habits spreading through the life of the congregation:

> Individuals' growth in confidence is also likely to be closely linked with the growth in discipleship amongst members of PMC churches that our survey identified. 71% of respondents said that PMC had had a significant or very significant impact on their discipleship…PMC is not primarily focused on individual discipleship but there are signs that PMC encourages collective and participatory acts and encourages higher individual involvement.[25]

Finally, in this chapter we must touch on the *systemic change* aspect of deciding to join in with what God is up to rather than asking God to bless our mission and outreach. Missional churches can together have a serious positive systemic effect on the whole church body that supports them. Just as the spiritual practices percolate or diffuse through the congregation it is important not to forget the two-way relationship local churches have with the body that supports them—in Anglican terms, the diocese. Once again, the TI report has important findings:

> This [the relationship of PMC and diocese] has to be understood as a two-way flow between churches and the wider diocese. In all of the cases considered, the diocese chose to be involved and provided funding for the churches. Dioceses also seem to have provided a necessary urgency to some churches, particularly those that were struggling, so that they participated. Although this suggests a proactive approach, it seems that dioceses have sometimes led but in other cases have simply allowed space for the process.

Bishops have an important role to play in encouraging PMC as a process as well as spreading its practices. Several dioceses have examples of holy habits from PMC being used more widely, including by bishops, for instance in diocese-wide gatherings of priests or laity. This suggests that at least some elements of PMC are gaining traction beyond the churches that have participated—an influence on the broader system.[26]

## 'How the Clergy-Lay Relationship Changed Through PMC'

We had a vicar who was very keen that we became involved with PMC and who was very supportive. She was good at discerning what people were good at and helping people to grow into their gifts. As a result, there are people who are doing things that they never thought possible. We always had a good group of lay people who were working within the church, but, as is usual, the same few were doing most of the work. The bulk of PMC work must, and is, done by lay people, but not the ones who are lay ministers. People are not only working behind the scenes now, but are being much more visible in their work. The vicar was able to join in with what we are doing, rather than always being the one in charge and leading everything, but at the same time prayerfully supporting all that we were doing. I say 'was,' because we now find ourselves in vacancy and, because we have learned so much through PMC, we are in a good place to work together to prepare our parish profile, we already know a lot about ourselves, our communities and what we want for our future. We are new to this vacancy thing, but we feel that PMC will help us through.

Maureen Garner, The United Benefice of Blidworth and Rainworth, Diocese of Southwell and Nottingham

## Reflection Question

- Where does the vision for your local church rest and how might more people come to embody it in their lives?

# 6 What Does Good Look Like in Missional Churches?

We are in a position as we come to the end of this book to sum up and bring together the answers to the question in our title. As we said at the beginning missional church is hard to define and is definitely not one thing; thus I have six brief headings that summarize what good looks like for us.

### Focused first and foremost on God, the three-in-one, who is community

The church begins and ends in God and God's mission; the overflow of love poured out in creation and redemption. Missional churches recognize the glory of God both in their worship and their worlds. They can name what God is up to in public so that other people can notice it too.

### Habitually forming Christian community around God's mission in the world

As missional churches discern God's activity, they are able to form new Christian community with the sending Spirit who also animates the people of peace they meet. They are therefore not busy, anxious or distracted. Since they can discern what God is up to, they have the freedom to say 'No' to good things.

### Authorizing public Christian witness and action in communities

In a context of privatized and individualized religion missional churches break out of this straitjacket by authorizing their people collectively to witness to their faith and take action in public. They know how to engage others in meaningful public relationships for the good of all. They are not shy of speaking of their faith and nurturing it in others towards a public profession. They make an appreciable and appreciated impact in their communities.

### Embodying an enduring long-term vision, which is embedded in God's people

God has a preferred and promised future for each local church which embodies the gospel in each church's own time and place. Missional churches articulate this vision that is also detailed and practical—able to be lived out day-by-day by the majority of members.

### Empowering people—influencing and supported by the wider church

Churches are systems and can be changed both locally and as whole-church bodies. Becoming missional is a process of diffusion of innovation which percolates slowly through the people—empowering them to join in the activity of God. God's people are liberated and set free through missional church.

### Learning how to learn and face the pain of change and conflict

Failure is not a problem for missional churches—by learning failures can become an excellent thing. With every action taken, reflected upon and the learning articulated churches can face a raising of the missional temperature. Levels of pain and conflict that they would have shied away from in the past can be faced and moved through with grace.

There is no panacea or silver bullet for the way the church's place is changing in Western society. However, in concluding this book we can say that missional church as an innovative way of being church does give us, I believe, a real, tangible and sustainable future in the face of decline and even the possibility of death.

# Notes

1 P Keifert and N Rooms; *Forming the Missional Church: Creating Deep Cultural Change in Congregations* (Grove Pastoral booklet P139).

2 P Keifert and N Rooms, *Spiritual Leadership in the Missional Church* (Grove Leadership booklet L38).

3 Available at https://churchmissionsociety.org/churches/partnership-missional-church

4 Available at https://churchmissionsociety.org/churches/partnership-missional-church/what-people-say-about-partnership-for-missional-church/ (hereafter TI report).

5 *ibid*, p 5.

6 P Keifert and N Rooms, *Forming the Missional Church: Creating Deep Cultural Change in Congregations* (Grove Pastoral booklet P139).

7 TI report, *op cit*, p 10.

8 'People of peace' is a phrase drawn from Luke 10, the sending of the 72—which seems to illustrate the *missio Dei* in action as we described in *Forming the Missional Church: Creating Deep Cultural Change in Congregations, op cit* (p 16). God's peace in the disciples is met graciously and hospitably by some (and only some) of those they are sent to, thus offering criteria for discerning where God is at work.

9 The 'House of Pain' wrestling club features in a video made by CMS about the PMC process and can be accessed at https://churchmissionsociety.org/churches/partnership-missional-church/

10 TI report, *op cit*, p 17; my emphasis.

11 The original seminal study in the UK with 511 participants is by John Finney in *Finding Faith Today: How Does it Happen?* (Swindon: Bible Society, 1992). The results are remarkably similar to a recent US study using the same methodology by Bryan Stone in *Finding Faith Today* (Eugene, OR: Cascade, 2018) with a sample size of 1,149.

12 *Forming the Missional Church, op cit.*

13 See Charles Taylor, *A Secular Age* (Cambridge MA: Harvard University Press, 2007).

14 To coin a phrase from the title of Bevans and Schroeder's 2011 key book on contemporary mission published by Orbis.

15 http://www.ottoscharmer.com/theoryu

16 In the Impact Evaluation research a 16% drop-out across the 82 participating churches was noted.

17 A programme sets specific targets and delineates step by step how to reach them. We do believe God has a preferred and promised future for each local church, but

we do not think it is a straight line to get there and we have no idea what it will look like since each context in which God is at work is entirely different.

**18** There is interesting data on this question of language in the evaluation report as we often receive pushback on the language we use. While we do not obfuscate deliberately and are very open to local translations being created we recognize the difficulty this represents for many participants.

**19** '*Living for Jesus'* is the missional vocation statement for Charlotte's church which emerged for them during the third year of the PMC process.

**20** *Spiritual Leadership in the Missional Church, op cit.*

**21** Keith Lamdin, *Finding your Leadership Style* (London: SPCK, 2012).

**22** See, for example, Nancy T Ammermann, *Congregation and Community* (New Brunswick, NJ: Rutgers UP, 1997).

**23** TI report, *op cit*, p 17.

**24** TI report, *op cit*, p 13.

**25** TI report, *op cit*, p 13.

**26** TI report, *op cit*, pp 18–19.